Coloring Fun with
THE THINK, THEN DO KARATE KID

KARATE DOJO

A companion coloring book to the children's picture book
"The Think, Then Do Karate Kid: A Dojo Kun Character Book
On Controlling Impulsiveness"

by Jenifer Tull-Gauger

ISBN-13 979-8-9866050-6-7

Youth Literary League

www.JeniferTullGauger.com

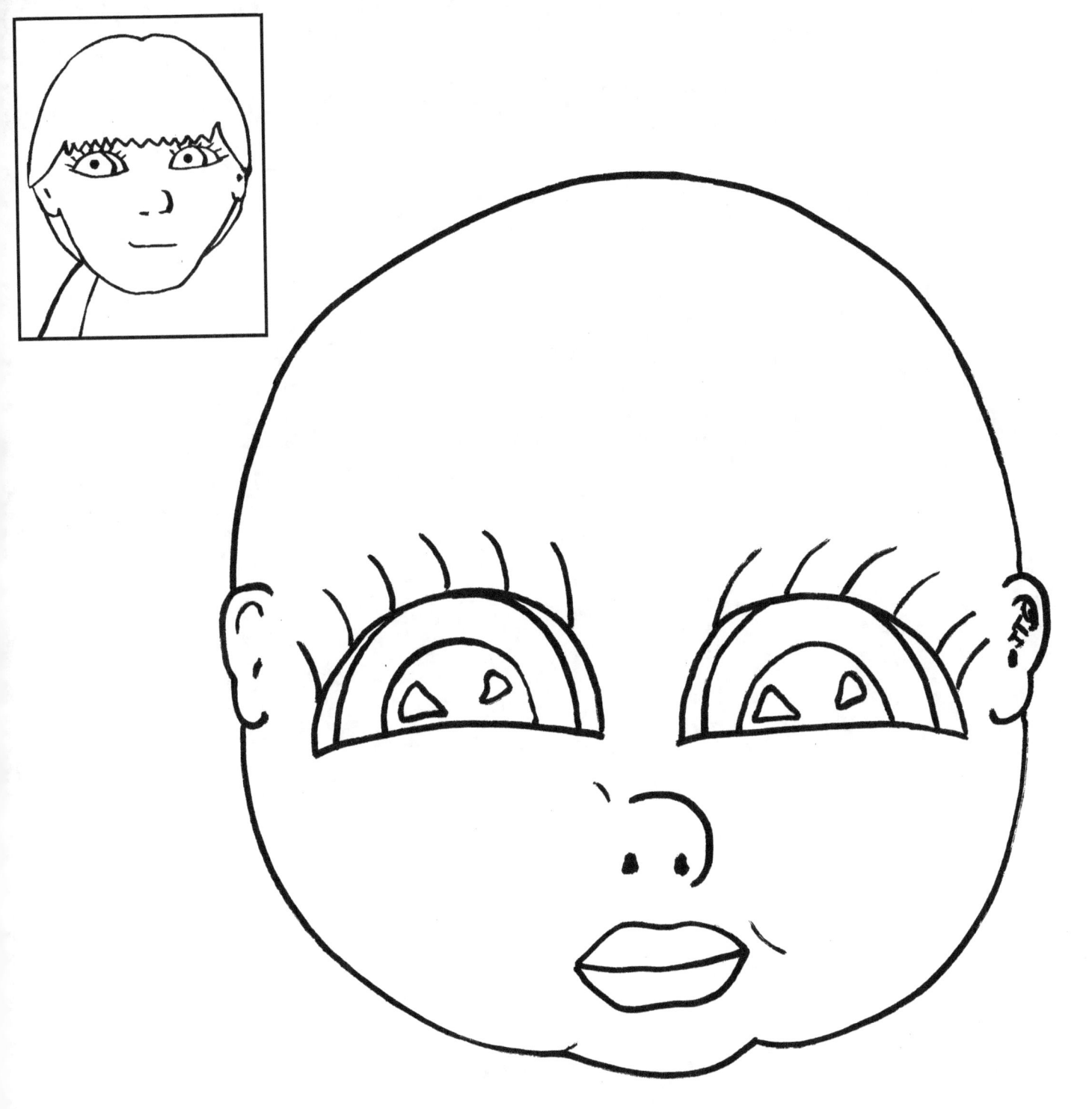

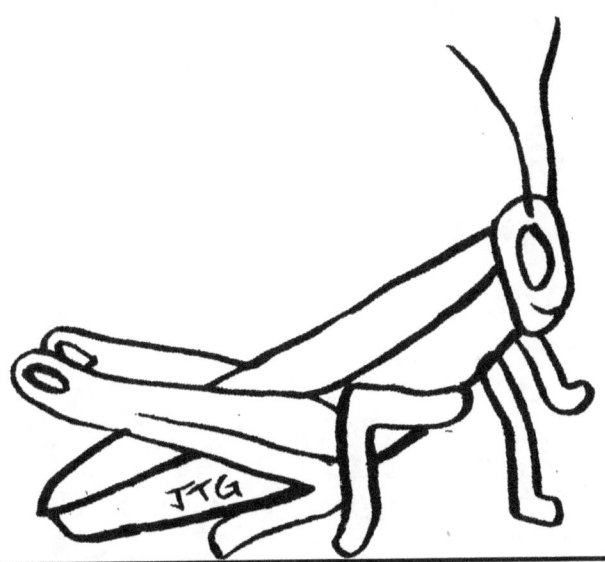

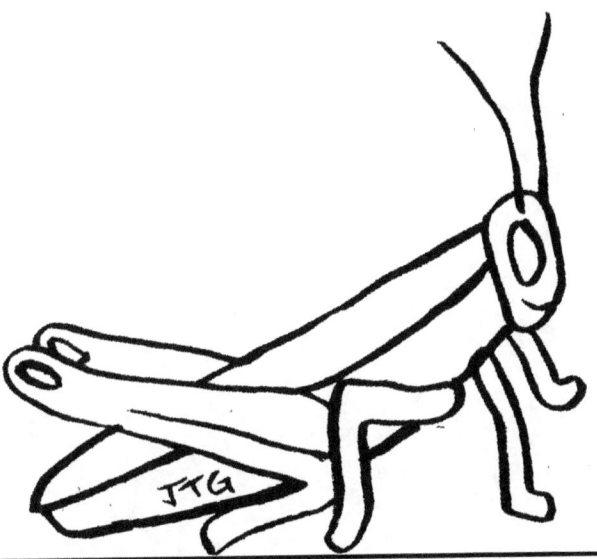

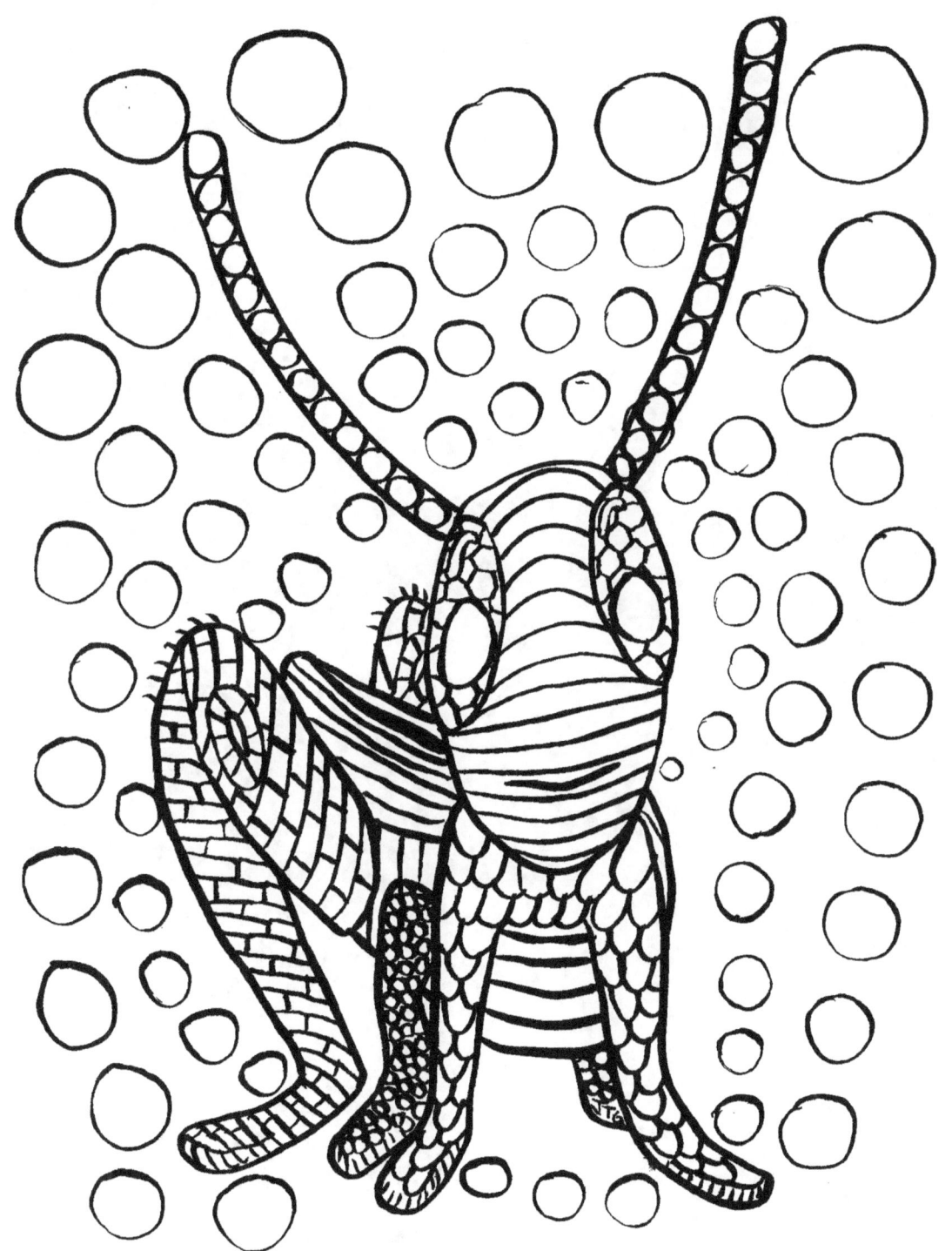

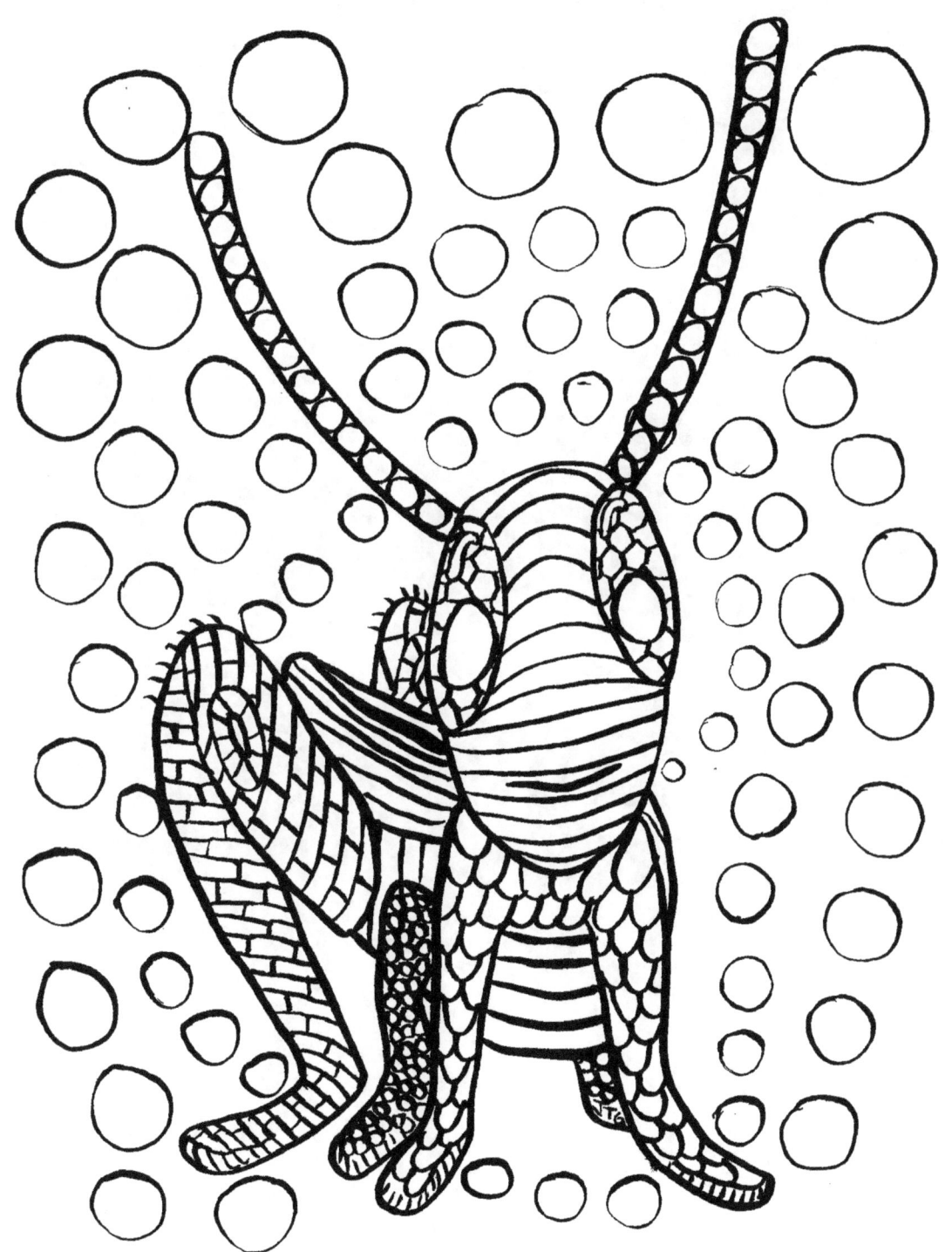

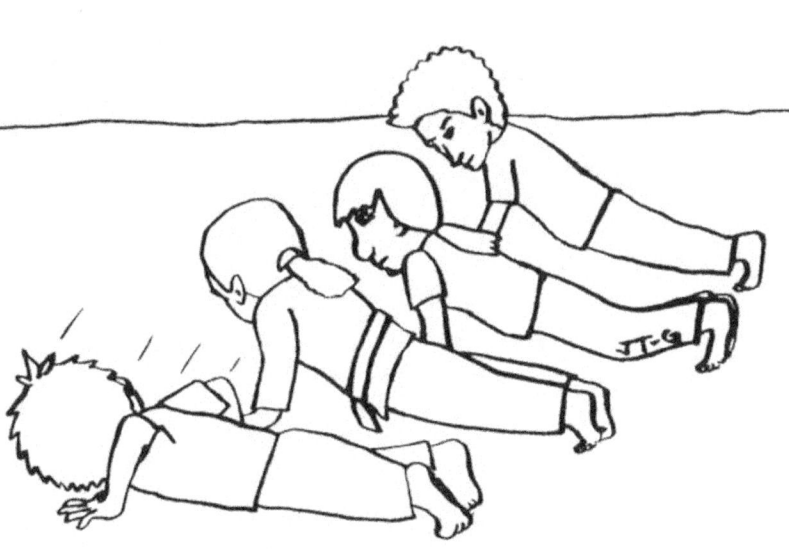

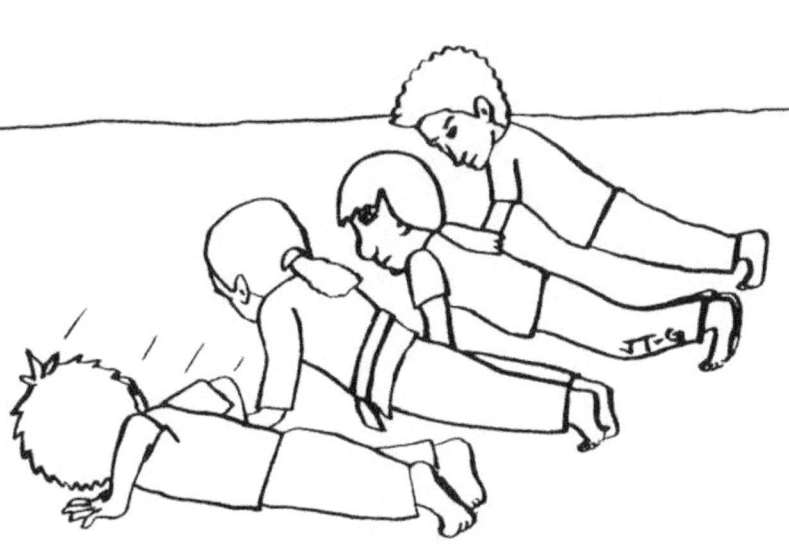

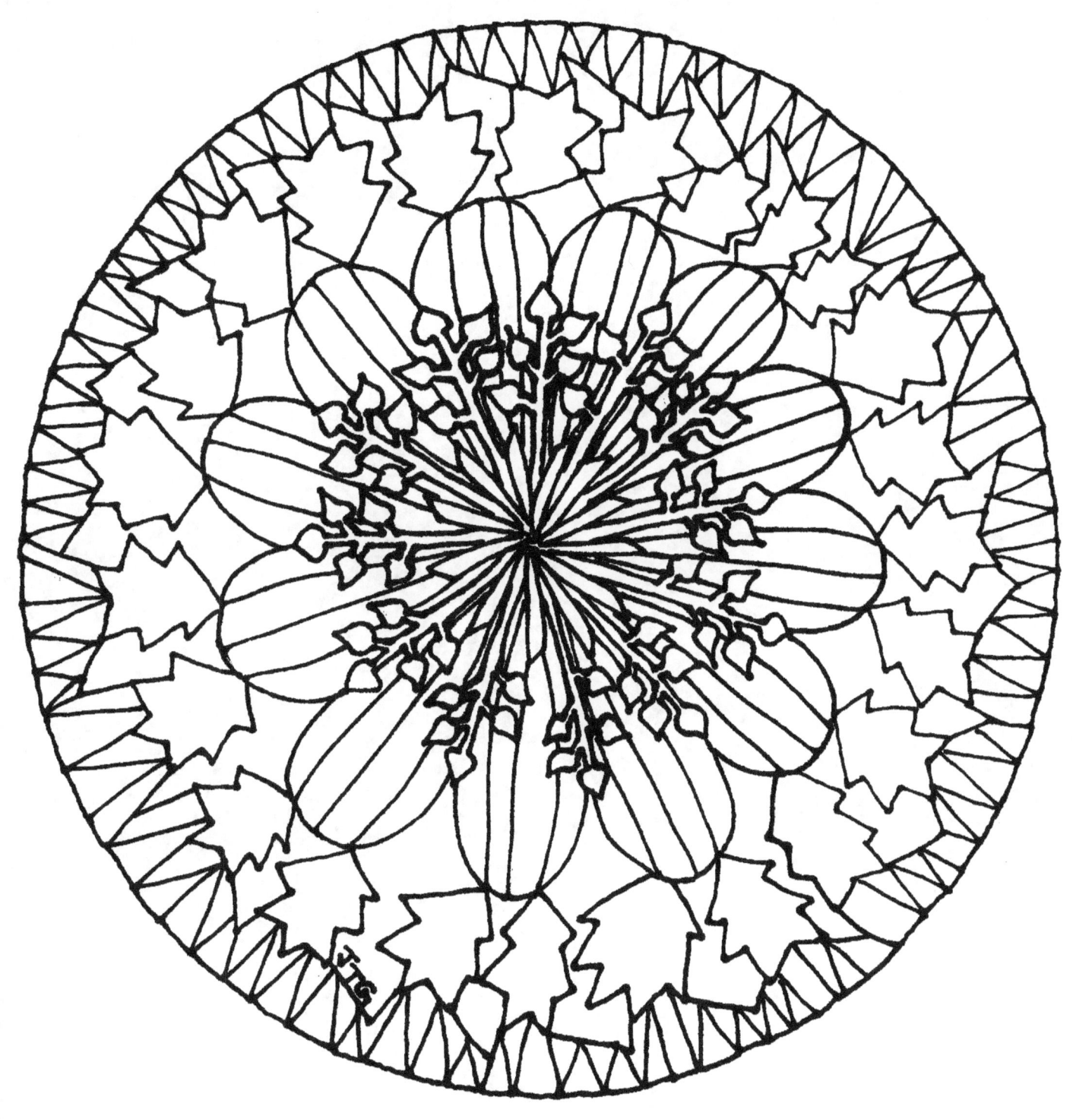

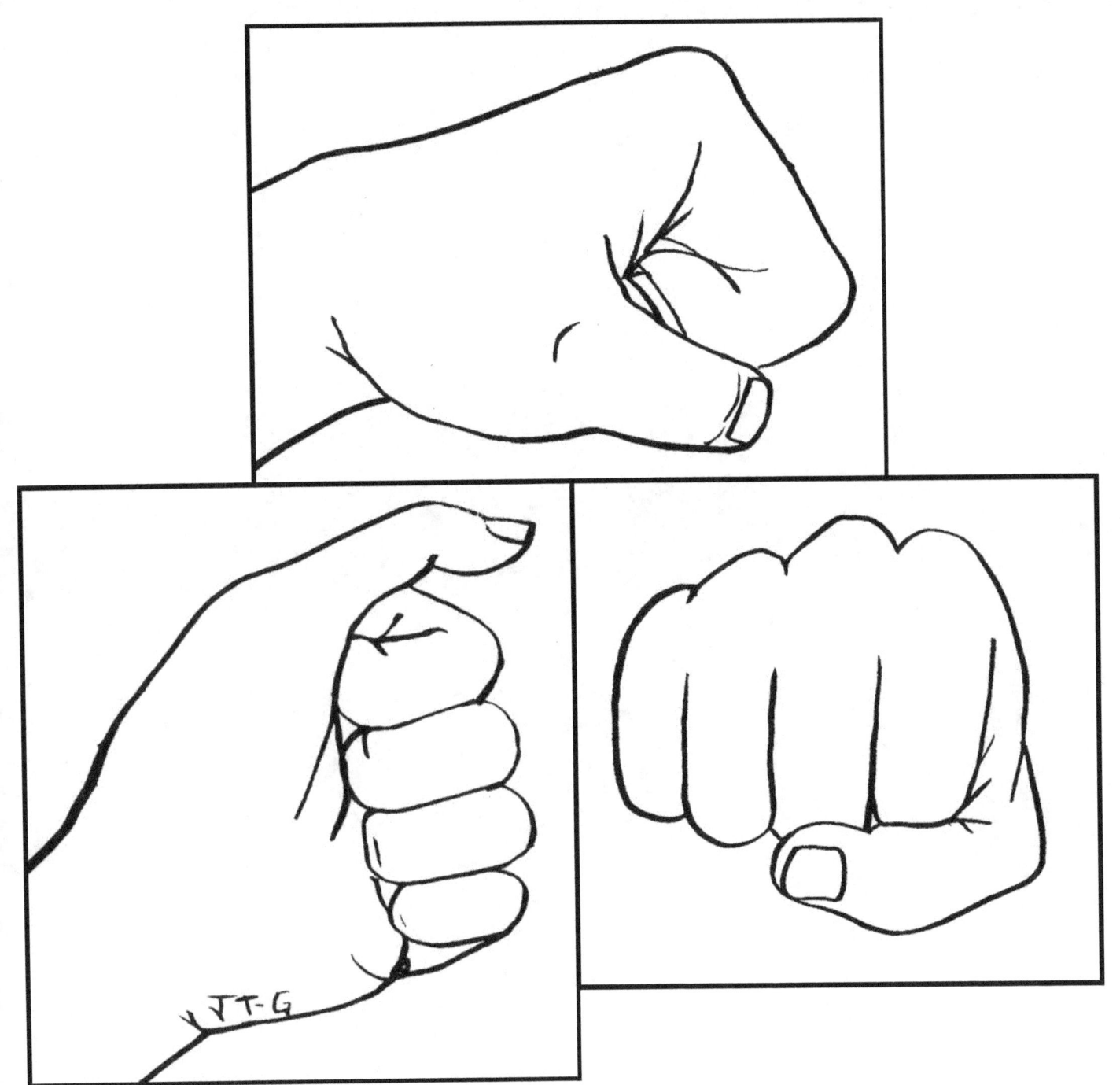

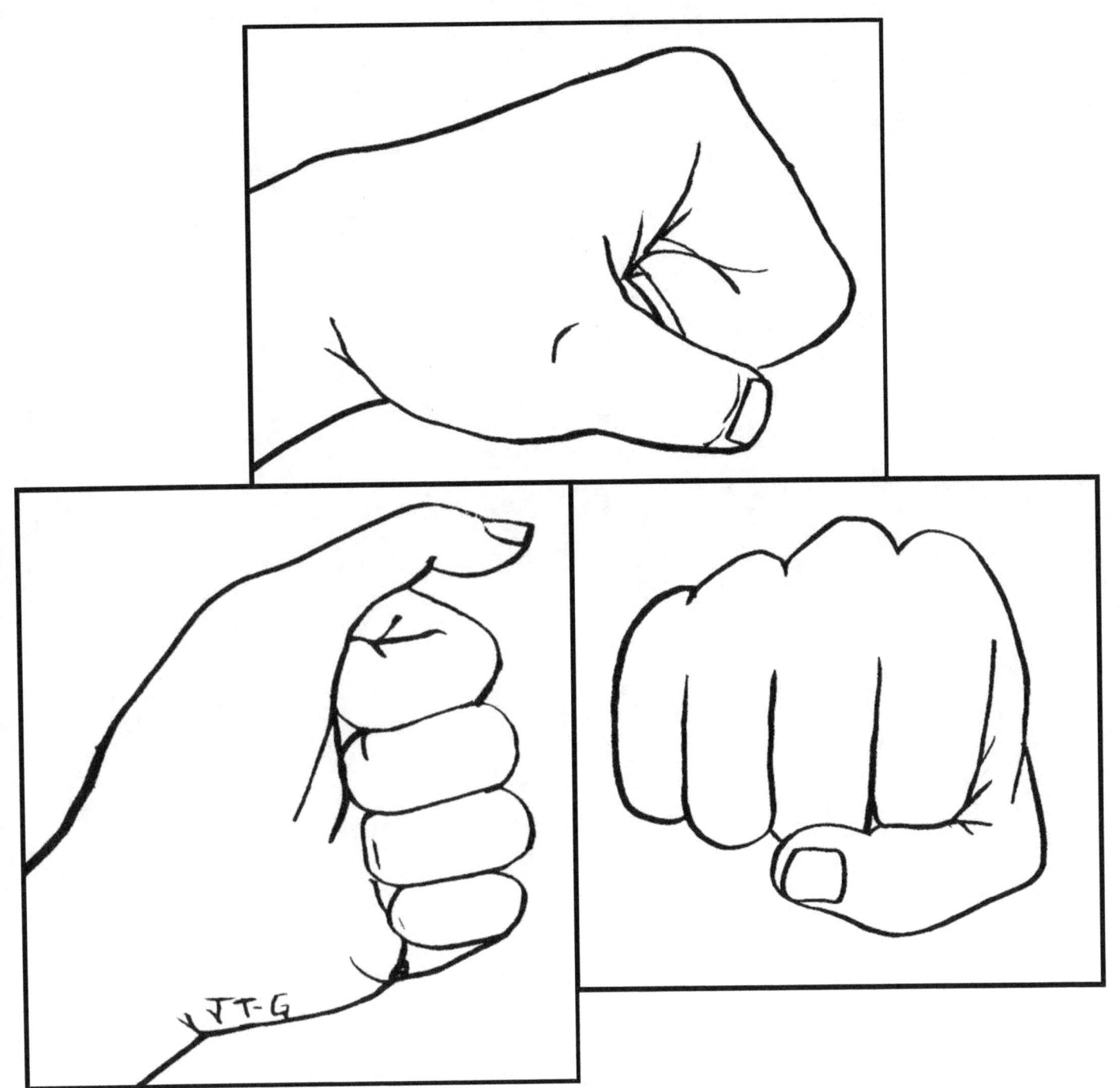

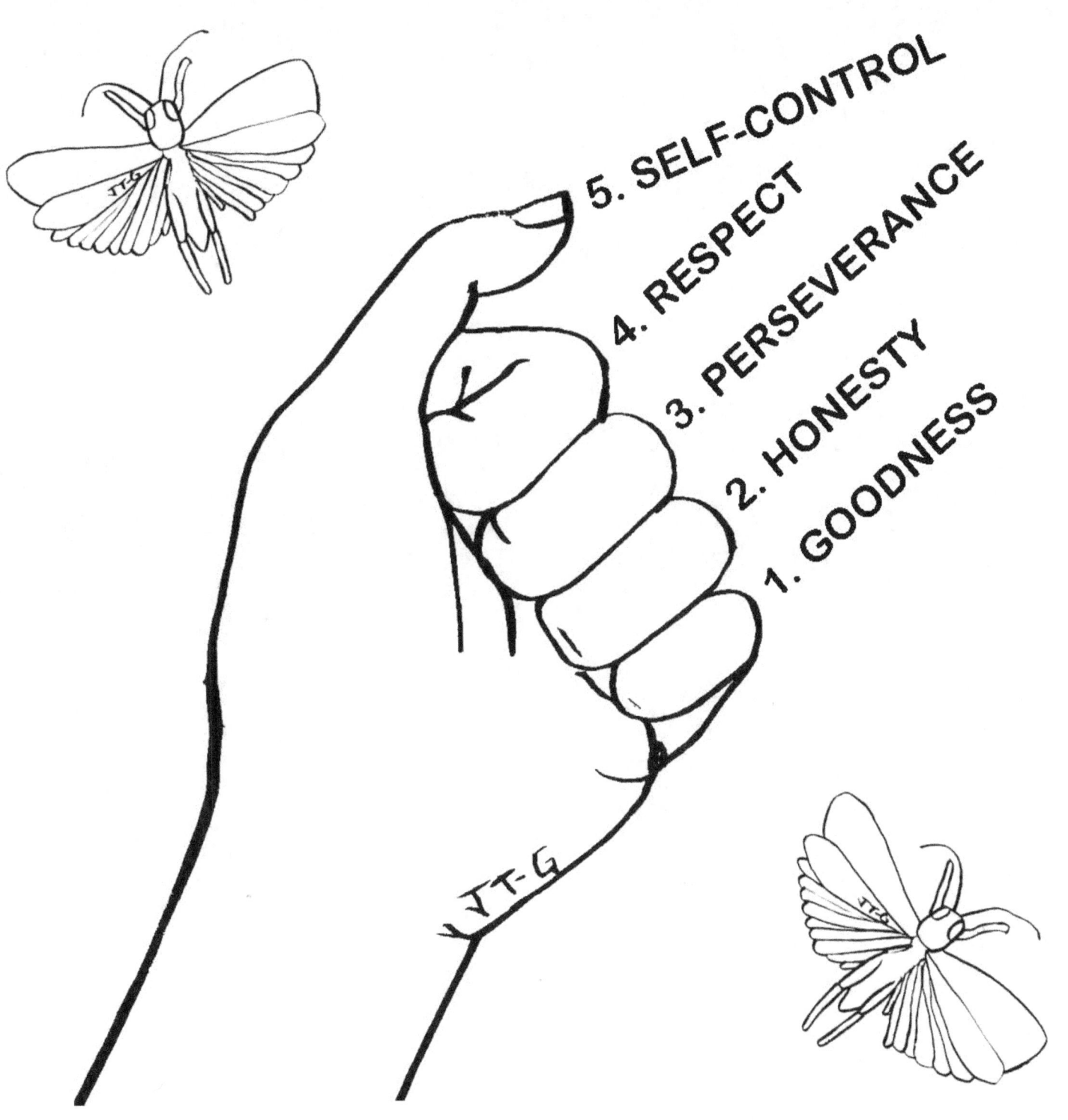

5. SELF-CONTROL
4. RESPECT
3. PERSEVERANCE
2. HONESTY
1. GOODNESS

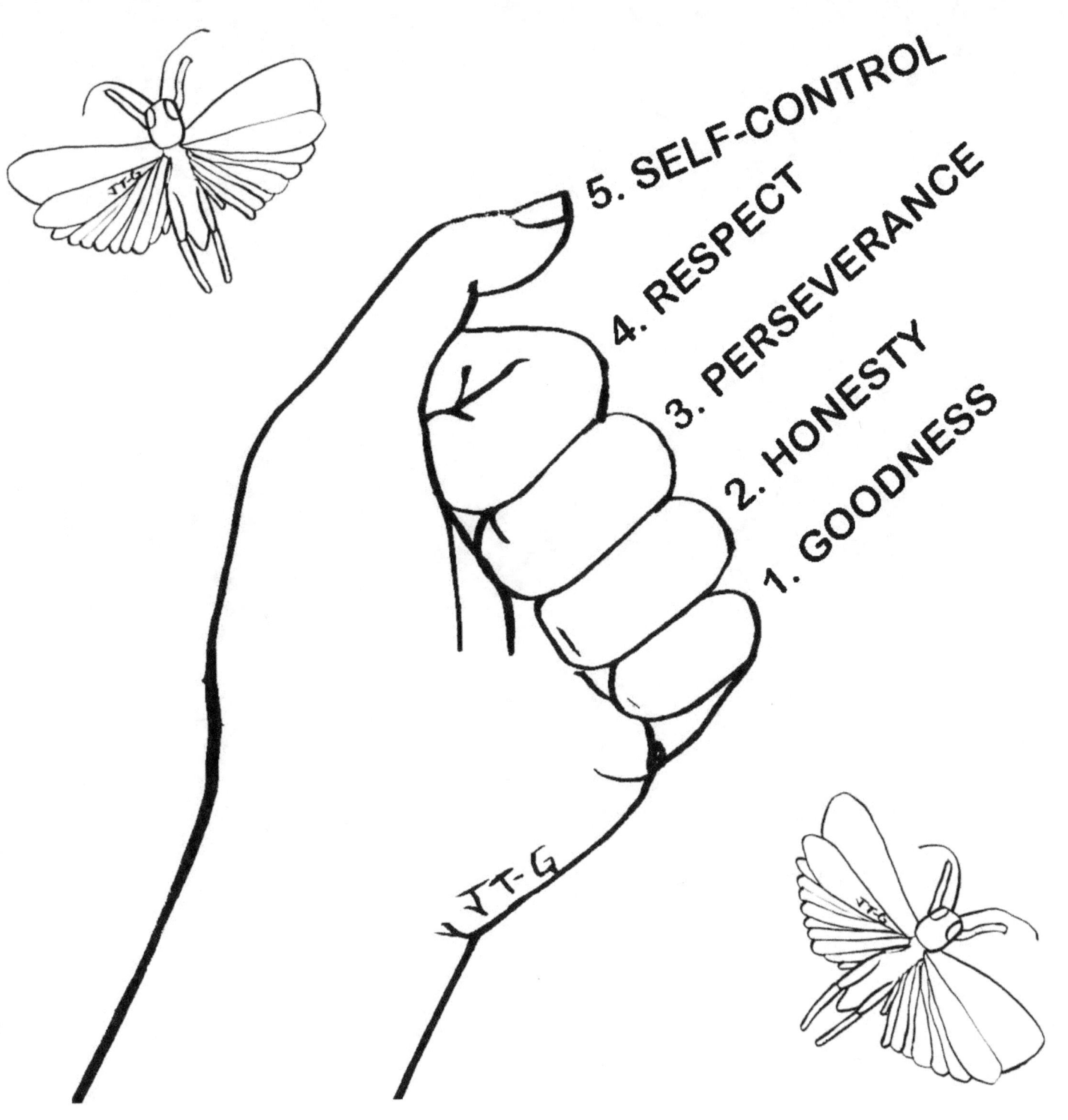

5. SELF-CONTROL
4. RESPECT
3. PERSEVERANCE
2. HONESTY
1. GOODNESS

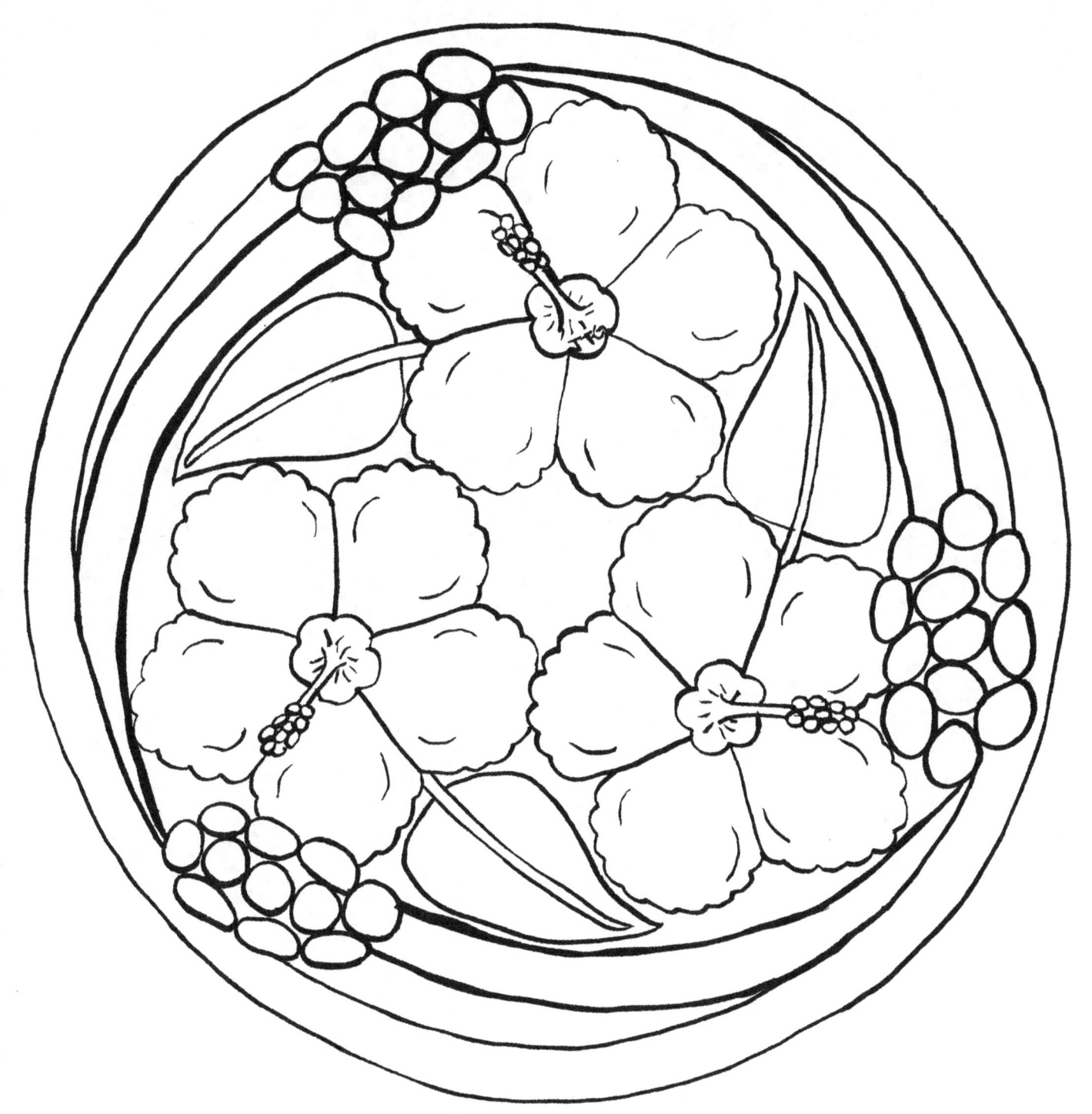

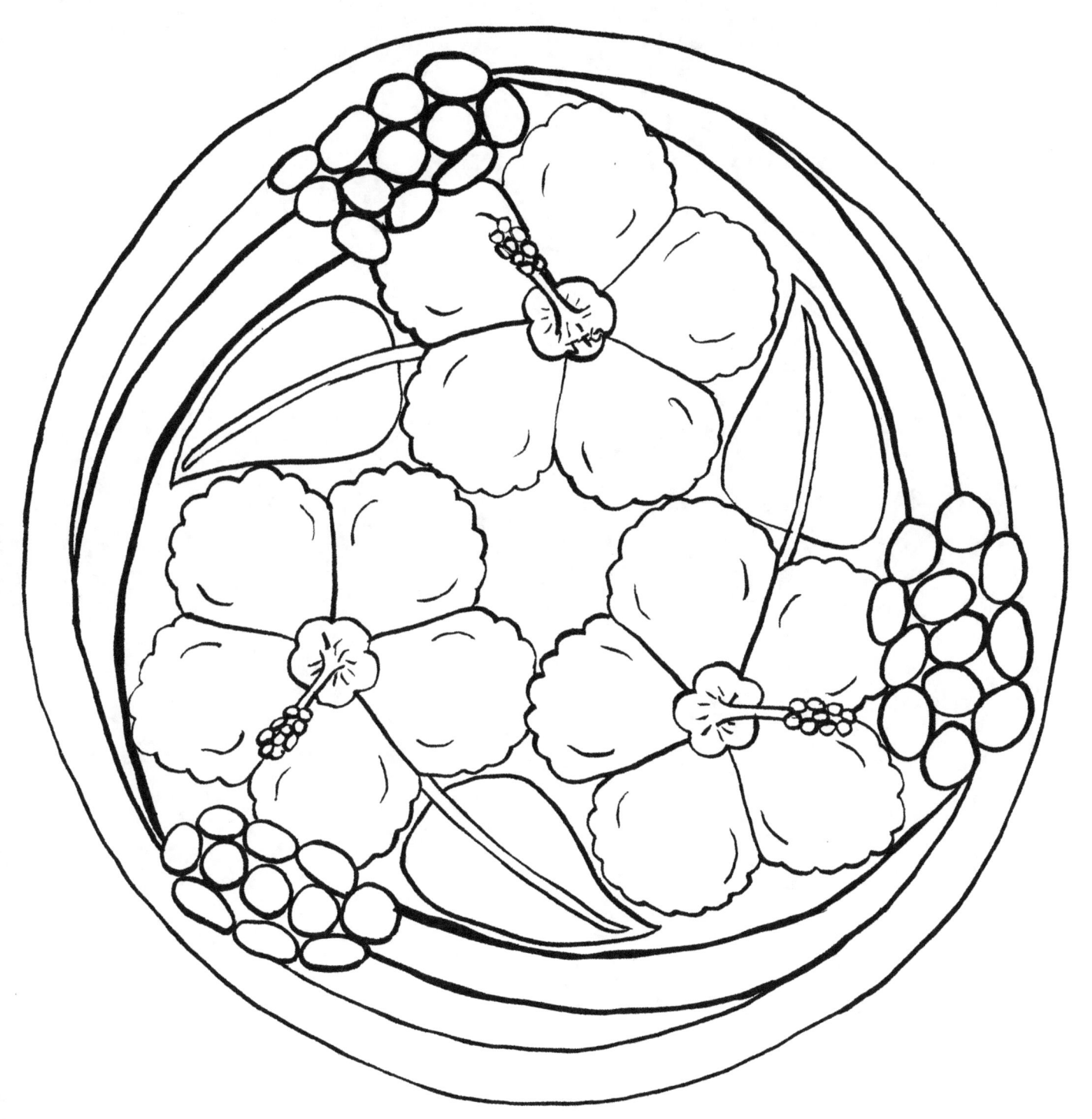

Read the Whole Story
Check out "The Think, Then Do Karate Kid: A Dojo Kun Character Book On Controlling Impulsiveness," a full-color children's picture book written and illustrated by Jenifer Tull-Gauger, available now on Amazon, BarnesandNoble.com, other websites, or by request at bookstores and libraries.

About Jenifer Tull-Gauger:
Jenifer loves to write stories and draw the pictures to make them into books. Her pictures and writings have appeared in several publications. Jenifer also loves karate. She trains in the traditional Okinawan karate style Ryukyu Kempo and teaches it to kids and adults.